Everything I have ever dreamed of
or remembered
exists somewhere

~ Angelo Letizia

Recent Publications by Angelo Letizia

Letizia, A.J.(2020) Graphic novels as pedagogy in social studies: How to draw citizenship. New York, NY; Palgrave-MacMillan Press.

Letizia, A.J. (2018) Using servant leadership: How to reframe the core functions of higher education, New Brunswick, NJ: Rutgers University Press.

Letizia, A.J. (2017) Democracy and social justice education in the information age. New York, NY: Palgrave-Macmillan Press.

Also by Angelo Letizia

Pilgrims of Infinity
    Silver Bow Publishing 2022

The Starry Devil and Other Unwanted Poems
    Silver Bow Publishing 2021

We Are the Winding Down

by

Angelo Letizia

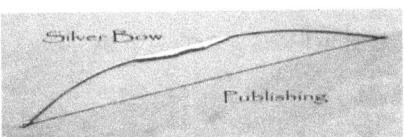

720 – Sixth Street, Box # 5
New Westminster, BC
V3C 3C5   CANADA

Title: We Are the Winding Down
Author: Angelo Letizia
Cover Art: "And the Lord Said, Let There Be Light"
    painting by Candice James
Layout and Design: Candice James
Editor: Candice James

All rights reserved including the right to reproduce or translate this book or any portions thereof, in any form without the permission of the publisher. Except for the use of short passages for review purposes, no part of this book may be reproduced, in part or in whole, or transmitted in any form or by any means, electronically or mechanically, including photocopying, recording, or any information or storage retrieval system without prior permission in writing from the publisher or a licence from the Canadian Copyright Collective Agency (Access Copyright).

www.silverbowpublishing.com
info@silverbowpublishing.com
© Silver Bow Publishing 2022
ISBN: 9781774032213 book
ISBN: 9781774032220 e book

Library and Archives Canada Cataloguing in Publication

Title: We are the winding down / by Angelo Letizia.
Names: Letizia, Angelo, author.
Description: Poems
Identifiers: Canadiana (print) 20220253250 | Canadiana (ebook) 20220254257 | ISBN 9781774032213
   (softcover) | ISBN 9781774032220 (EPUB)
Classification: LCC PS3612.E79 W4 2022 | DDC 811/.6—dc23

Foreword

This book is about failure. But not a personal failure. It is about failure in an existential sense. What does it mean for a people or a society to fail? And if a society does fail, how long does it take? Do its people know they are failing? Did the Romans know they were in decline? What actually constitutes a failure? In a wider sense, this might sound like end times or end of the world talk. And in some sense it is. But this notion of end times needs some clarification. There is more than one way to think about the end of the world. The end of the world can be thought of in linear terms, from a defined starting and end point. This is reminiscent of the Judeo-Christian world view, where God created the world and where he will one day destroy it. So maybe this is it, end times. Or one could take a more cyclical view, where the universe is seen in perpetual motion, going through cycles of creation and destruction, like in the Hindu vision. And perhaps we're at the cusp of one of its destructions. And to be fair, at many times in history, many people have lamented that we as a species were living in end times but the end never seems to come. Perhaps I am no different, perhaps people like me are the appointed criers of history which must signal end times every so often only to be laughed at later. However, the specter of nuclear warfare has added a new and deadly twist to the end time's argument (and as I write this, the war in Ukraine rages on which has brought back the terrifying prospect of nuclear destruction).

But let's assume that perhaps I am wrong and we are not living through end times. If this is the case, then I argue that maybe we *should* be living through end times. Failure is heightened when the entity that fails has tremendous potential. We as a species have tremendous potential. We have done some great and splendid things, from our literary, mechanical, engineering, transportation, communication and medical advances to name a few. But we are falling short, we as a species could feed, clothe, house and educate every individual on this planet with some work. We could do so much more but we become so mired in bullshit, so mired in tribal disputes, we use our technologies and insights for base and harmful things; we are conned by demagogues and strongmen who claim they can save us. And we want to be saved so badly and in this pursuit to be saved we destroy ourselves.

At no other time in history have we had this potential to make life better for our fellows, to truly live a meaningful life as individuals and a species. While meaning is subjective, we could try to create it together. And that is what makes me, and those like me, different than the ones in the past. In some sense, this book might be the voice of failure, of a lone being who somehow became cognizant of the failure of his society, of the lost potential. Perhaps we need the end, or at least *an* end to realize this.

We squandered our potential and should wait for the next evolution to bring something better. Perhaps then, the end is not Armageddon, it is not some god smiting us. No, perhaps *failure* is the end, our own preventable failure. It is a slow, painful death that we as a species do not realize we are living through. And when we finally fail, when we are finally gone, then maybe a new evolution, an overman or some infinite being might replace us, try again, and succeed where we have failed.

Pity we will not be able to see it.

Angelo J. Letizia, Manchester MD, April 1st, 2022

to my descendants far into the future.
I hope they can use it.

Table of Contents

Here at the end ... 11
Whimper ... 12
A room in the sun ... 13
The Ballad of Moses Hess ... 14
Star wax ... 15
Poetry at the end ... 16
Stupid gods ... 17
We create geniuses and idiots ... 18
Each letter is Jerusalem ... 19
Corners ... 20
The mundane ... 21
Prenatal galaxies ... 22
No place ... 23
The inevitable ... 24
7,056th homily ... 25
The slope and the grade ... 26
Is it there? ... 27
There is no light here ... 28
Synthetic big bang ... 29
On the way to the bank ... 30
Saluting killers ... 31
The great ... 32
Another salute ... 33
We are all Carthage ... 34
Rocks and bulwarks ... 35
An empirical nightmare ... 36
It's all here ... 37
Eschatology led us here ... 38
St. Pariah ... 39
The existential failure ... 40
In 1996 I read a book about the information superhighway ... 41
Harbors become pathogens ... 42
Anti-bacterial ... 43
Here ... 44
The swollen ... 45
Confession ... 46
The antichrist ... 48
Nirvana is you ... 49
The red paint fails ... 50

Hawk Mountain Sanctuary ... 51
The repose ... 52
Camping in the stars ... 53
Coffee spoons ... 54
Liminal failures ... 55
Beggars gesture between the stars ... 56
Reverse eschatology ... 57
Ammonia and turpentine ... 58
Human soil ... 59
Everything ... 60
Rebuild the Messiah ... 61
It did not have to happen this way ... 62
Accountability as helium ... 63
My friends ... 64
You have done it 6 times before (that I know of) ... 65
Progress mapped onto tombs ... 66
Ingested this life which dies ... 67
The same end ... 68
Thinking about the end (drinking poem) ... 69
Ballast ... 70
Receptacle ... 71
We are the only thing left (Objective end) ... 72
We should have seen it sooner (Subjective end) ... 73

Acknowledgments ... 74

Here at the end

There is only
And ever was
Only one way
And that is:
Through the stone, through the concrete
Through the steel
Through electrical current
Through the rubber and
Through the glass
Through the blood
And arriving here
At this place, and this moment in time

    II

In the beginning
There was nothing
But always with
The possibility of something
So it was never nothing
Nothing needed to make that possibility extinct
In order to truly be nothing
The possibility of something is teeth
Is metal and eyebrows
And concrete
The possibility of something is entropy
And it spends itself
Until nothing is nothing

    III

We are the winding down
We are the result
We are the powder and crumbs
The ash
The embers on the ground
We are the groans
It won't be long now-
I hope

Whimper

There are only a few workers now
Hunched over in offices
Those buildings become the only support
For the aging universe

The few send emails
And write reports
To keep busy
But no one reads them
The employees eat lunch in small groups
But rarely converse

They go home
Watch black and white reruns
On wood-paneled televisions
Their reward for surviving
The smoke
And false advertising

A room in the sun

There is a room in the sun
A bed and a rug on fire
There is a closet in the moon
All of my vacuums are stacked there

Dusty things that aborted my blood
Lifted it straight from the skull
And bed sheets and bathroom floor

And now this cosmic house suits me well
A planetary existence
Revolving suns and meteors
Seen through a telescope

In cold space
Where I freeze to particles
And frozen hairs above the lip
Dancing in silence

Coordinated movements of planets
Celestial patterns
That have me fixed
In this instant for eternity
In one forgotten moment in a classroom

With a dull pencil
Tallying on loose-leaf
The motion of the snow
As if my skin was shredded and bleached to confetti leaflets
Sprinkled to earth from an urn
In the sky I knew so well

The Ballad of Moses Hess

Maybe there is a utopia seed in all of us
In the ventricle or crowned tooth
The sticky marmalade of the heavens
Bends awkwardly around dreams
We have not had yet
Like the cracked enamel of our aspirations
The red and white sweaters of distinction
The endowed chairs
Forgotten concrete, all of these
The elite bastions of our indifference crumble
Welcome and stand
Welcome and persevere
Utopia is fully formed
And finally realized
As it sprouts from the clay

Star wax

I failed to extinguish the stars again
Those pitiless replicas
Which burn indifferently to all of our suffering
They are light-years away but
Jealously drip their crooked wax
Into coffee, sewers and dreams
That celestial paste however holds this universe together
Tightly, silently.
And against all known logic
Even logic joins the heart and the star
blood star wax runs through
Solar veins, I want to hate them
But how can I hate my own circulatory system?
Stars circulate in this blood while little doors are carved
Into the black of the universe on a summer night
For me, to claw through
Squeeze through the matter and be born
Into something new and far away
Something that smells of rain
And paint
And ideas I cannot name

Poetry at the end

Longitude laid over an ocean
Which is drained through the reef
Arctic ice sheets melted
Along with the equator
There is no more need for these things
There is no more poetry
At the end
Just sequence and gravity
Which whispers in the husk of the ozone

Stupid gods

The stars are cheese and honey
That a greedy stupid god ate
Then he planted the core of the earth
Which gives us bad thoughts
But we cannot get rid of it
So we live with it
Under our feet
And try to ignore all the bad dreams

We create geniuses and idiots

We create geniuses and idiots
Methods breed them like a fetus
Greasy membranes are
The secret of bureaucracy
I wish these things would fossilize
Because they might be a plague
In the corner
Washed through the gutter

How many more geniuses do you need?
How many more celebrities must burn?
Where are all the genocides? Siphoned through the sieve?
Or perhaps gestating sleeping dreaming?

There is a hole in the shoe
Whisky drains through past the sole
But these shoes are creased and old
Leathery smell wafts in the closet
A universe of wood and dust
A universe unto itself

We need more geniuses
And more idiots
And one more fetus
To grow a better civilization
Than the one we celebrate now
Which still needs its gods

Each letter is Jerusalem

Opaque ghosts resurrect in mailboxes
Relive their deaths
And their red tongues
Are still wet
They are panting and spitting

Hungry ghosts stalk veins
In four lane highways
These goddam things are everywhere
The stars are ghosts
And so is the core of the earth
They are always there
And they replace the things I love
One by one
A procession of ghosts
Marches by in unison
In boots and parades
Eating with plastic forks
Looking up at me and then back
To their cold noodles

Corners

Perforated streets
And corners
Separate into oceans
Voids of expanse
Useless as concrete
Expanding into black
Into little paper strips
Which hang off its metal rings
Like a partial abortion
Between one world and
The next

The mundane

The shag carpet is familiar
So is the mildew smell
It is comforting
One floor is placed over another
Little oceans over the core
Roll up the green yards
We need a new ground

Prenatal galaxies

Stars are umbilical cords
Surrounded by marrow
And we, the primitive surgeons
Gleefully hack the ruins
But we miss the bone miss the core and
Miss all the conduits
Which gestate symbols and fetuses
Silent orbits become
A eulogy of sorts
Revolving us
Into a phyla of ignorance

No place

We are what once was
Never what is or
What becomes
There are no more
Dreams here
No more possibilities
And no more utopias
There are only cornhusks
Rolled flat
Cracked and splintered
Into dust

Nothing grows here
Nothing ever will

There is nowhere to meet
Nowhere to go
There is just
Just

The inevitable

Can you break a sky?
That false covering gives no hope
Broken open
The only shield
We have
And let me walk
Without mediation
Without hindrance
From that dead symbol

7,056th homily

Liturgical grass
Grows like a sermon
To sooth tongues and ears
Spoken fertilizer
Calms insurance rates
There is a stock market
In the vein
But you cannot win
At this voodoo
It is rigged
It's out of your control
The wax ring of the toilet
Seals the shit, but its
Not tight enough
There are too many
Apocalypses gestating
And too many traffic lights
Telling me what to do
Instructing
The stock market yield curves too
They tell me

The slope and grade

I make teachers
Audio cancers or floating graves
We can grade the eye
But not stop the downward plane
Which descends into disbelief
Where is the utopia we were promised?
There is only stale bread
And granite countertops
And endless fiberglass
What a waste
We could have been so much more
At least
That is what we were taught
But the teachers read that in a book
Now we are just here
With nothing to do
Walking mouthing truths
To anyone who will disbelieve
Trusting those truths
And believing we are free
This is not defendable
Nor should it be
We cannot sustain the rubber tires
And IPADS
We cannot foresee
All we
Were supposed to become

Is it there?

I will eat the universe
Suck her vitamins
From each corner and piston
There are so many secret nutrients
In this universe
Which beg to be consumed
You just have to know
Where to look
I can taste the dead star
In her rectum
And the liberating soundwaves
Which slice the atmosphere
Into unnatural funnels and digestive tracts
Passages for all those nutrients
Locked in wax rings and
Roofing shingles
And in the patch of trees
In the middle of some highway
Where all the vestigial prefrontal cortexes
Go to become obsolete
Eventually

There is no light here

There is no light here
Even though the sun shines
And a lamp is on
Perhaps the light is hiding
Refusing to guide
Refusing to show the way
To people who ignore it

There are no more continents
But maybe one is in the closet
A virginal land
Of dust and hardwood floors
Where there is no light
We will just explore
In the dark then

Man-made big bang

I love the smell of bleach
It reminds me
Of how clean
We try to be
Bleach reaches into the atmosphere
And scrubs the universe
Of its dead stars
We don't need them anymore
Disinfect the blood and rotors
Strip them of color
Slice their rubber through
Disinfectant is the agent of revolution
To make the universe
Clean and new

On the way to the bank

There is a space between two houses
Where a crooked shadow sleeps
Oblong contours outline
Outdated vinyl siding
In an ecstasy of existential geometry
Shadows, corners and angles meet
To frame the scraps of our aspirations
Which have been reborn into sins

Saluting Killers

They must be bored again
Thinking of all the times they died
And buying cheap plastic flags
With chipped paint
To mark the solemn occasion
Boil the stars to paste
Chase with a shot of whiskey
You will need it for this memorial
For its hypocrisy and folded cardboard replicas
That become trash
And line the memory
Like so many guttural things

The great

Atoms and orphans swim in ammonia
In chiseled noise
Like an exoskeleton
Outstretched
To form a constellation of sorts
Which pivots on some invisible point
In the bleached universe
And ascends like fumes
Like a pantomime
A prelude to something better
Something useful
A brand new immune system
Which inoculates the stars and hemorrhages DNA
On some distant ocean floor so
Pathogens can renew themselves
Infinitely, and grow stronger
And pierce the silhouettes
Of slain teleology's
Patterns of debris
Come to rest on our ambitions
And become vertebrates

Another salute

You must be bored
That's why you bought
That cheap plastic flag
(while children are hungry)
Flying it
Gives you something to do
Something to be
Bald tires tread
On a worn road
Glass is like confetti
To celebrate your meaning

We are all Carthage

A ruined pedagogy
Instructs a curriculum of debris
Squeezing the flash
Of momentary light
That is also a momentary and fleeting guide
And shines it
Into windows that wrap around the grass
But the grass has salt in it now
Where nothing grows
But we don't need growth anymore

Rocks and bulwarks

Temporary appendages
Guard against entropy
No matter how many guillotines you erect
The tar oozes
You cannot slice its viscous heart
The tar just dulls the blade
And rain downs
Like slow blood
On the ground
To remind you how useless
Your rocks and bulwarks are

An empirical nightmare

Withered wax can never be shrapnel
It is just an accident
A type of cylindrical blackmail
Furnished for the sanctity of your insurrection
An empirical nightmare
With no mathematical solution
Only atoms left untended
To become an antichrist
An eternal thing to hate
To be relevant when needed
An antichrist which can kill all of our vernaculars
And all of our well-meaning accidents

It's all here

Segments resistant to decay
Are now fossilized silhouettes
Which foolishly still have ambitions
And become
The tenets of a new ideology
Bestowed on oak doors
And coral and vortexes
Where weather systems meet
Tree bark becomes a cipher
A living hieroglyph
To tell the story of a forgotten people
And their artificial rituals
Of failure and acceptance

Eschatology led us here?

The pilgrims and ambassadors sit quietly
One tends the fire
There are so many things
Their brothers could have been
They had so much potential
But now
There is only the next evolution to look forward to
And so the pilgrims whisper
Their final prayer

St. Pariah

Your leprosy flowers in the chalk
And it continues to intoxicate
And sacrifice itself infinitely
But there is only pain now
No harbors or formulas
We mourn for a hallucination
Which drops an arm
Scraps of what it used to be
Which dissolve into light and equinoxes
Dwarf stars with open mouths
And toothless grins
Welcome all the lepers
Preserved in their shallow mausoleums
And symbolic structures

The existential failure

Delegate the instruments so
The jawbone yardstick
Has its vernacular
To escape the borders of flesh and mathematics
But a leaky rhetoric paves the ground
In mirrors
Which flattens the grass
But ensures a
Flat surface and
Perpendicular sins
Become atoms
On which to build and constitute
A new reality

In 1996 I read a book about the information superhighway

Information is asphalt
And cement
An artery bent around a streetlight
In some memory
Arties connect
The internal and the external
Over a server
Modem in blood
Runs into an oil pan
Where your schemas are greased
And jammed into a star
The now silent infrastructure

Harbors become pathogens

Harbors become pathogens
Divorce the inscription from the exodus
And sow a voyage without words
We are the weary savages
Dying in a foreign land
We still call home

A refraction of the grotesque
Seems logical now
As it glimmers in the cinders
Of what we used to love
Cinders like gods
Shoveled over in despair

Anti-bacterial

The procedure is immune
Like a jawless symmetry
Which is washed on an altar
There is annihilation waiting in that symmetry
The trophy for living
A crooked exoskeleton
Which doubles as a grotesque memorial
That the stupid pray to

Here

The rain reminds me
Of our primeval heritage
Of dried blood and fashioned stones
Of a mottled leaf
Which eventually rots
And leaves its sweet smell
Clinging to the mossy wheel
A grinding thing of certainty
A slow hum of stone on stone
Of the pitiless wheel
Which burns cold
Like a stone sun
A monotonous god
In some desolate but beautiful forest
Which comes to life
Among the oaks

The swollen

Solitary scythes
Summon the chimera
Braided guillotine in barren nerves
This spectacle is redeemed in the syllable
A relic of
A different methodology
A howling vertical density
Vinegar and the witness
Indigenous and anonymous crusaders
Which breach the boundaries of sacrifice

Confession

Why do I brush my teeth?
Cleanse the bones
Preserve the soul
I am not afraid
To let them rot
And stink
Yellow and decay
Into medallions of detachment

My beard grows
Is clipped and shaven
Because I want to impress the girls
Big breasted and soft skinned
Woman who laugh
And fuck
And are not impressed
By me

Gathered in my living room
Palace of the mundane
Ruled by freaks
That I call friends
All kings and queens
Ruling each other in the world
On loan from logic

I have failed
What used to help me love
I've burnt it
Dancing around the fire
Offering to it
My heart
Torn out of my chest
Laughing
I tossed it in the flames
I knew no better

Take a ticket
See the freak
Ruling his kingdom
Brushing his teeth
Storing his tooth brush
Within the hole
Of his upright chest

The antichrist

The antichrist cannot evacuate
Because he is simulated
And six thousand copies of him
Now sit, bored with chapped lips
Fat on plagues
Which spread among the mundane grocery stores
Where there are
Guillotines in the aisles
But they cannot sever the voices from the copies
The frequency from the simulations
Dwarf gods limp
And can now relax
And laugh at us instead

Nirvana is you

A complacent Buddha sits in the Nepalese sun
And oh, how the stock markets shudder
Centuries later

Cameras are bolted to the telephone poles
Like gods eyes stapled to monsters
Watching us all squirm at the bottom

How many Buddhas walk here?
How many Satans drink coffee? Or maybe
The gods we created are laughing
Because we couldn't do it any better

We own new superstitions and zealots
hide in the produce aisle
Refrigerator hums like sermons
And salvation is refracted in the glass

The red paint fails

The red paint fails
So does the pine
And stars fail to shine
Burn
And guide
We are alone now
In a cold and colorless cave

Cigar ash blots the sun
Beer cans bob in the river lazily
They fail too
To build a new rock
To base this new church on
But this river
Is some sort of celestial artery
In the middle of Pennsylvania
A haven of sorts
For rotted branches in the lush canopy
Where the universe is twisted onto itself
Like new norths
Gateways in the bark

Hawk Mountain Sanctuary

A man built a little house on the riverbank
Where he drank the universe from a stream
And blessed the sound with his eyes
He walked in mud and made craters of the earth
Which vanished in the next rain storm
This is now his sky, his rain, his currency
But the fish still do not give up their secrets
Even when they leap up and momentarily
Break the back of the stream
There were dreams and cigar ashes and now just
A babbling god cold and wet which
Owned the sights and ate the mud
This is a sovereign kingdom
Built on the mossy rocks and fishhooks
Far away from logic

The repose

The abstract land is a shape
Smooth and glass
Cold to touch but
Enticing to some
Glass planes distill sands and light
To a single point, to a thought
Which can not materialize in most beasts
So they insult the glass
And burn it to turn back to sand
Because it is all they know

Camping in the stars

A prophet digs in the gorge
His words are hieroglyphs
For things you have not yet dreamt about
The river is his galaxy
His sanctuary
Shallow and cold
Where it gives birth
To your scripts
To your fleeting norths
Which you desperately cling to like gods
And yet
You still ignore him
But somehow he is your lynchpin

Coffee spoons

Measurement is
Disinfectant
Like a glass door
In sunset
Like a categorical imperative
Or
The impermanence of corners
Wrapped around marble
Mountains in the distance
Are a sort of hieroglyph
A daily Pentecost
To paralyze the remaining sinners

Liminal failures

What about the ones with small beaks
That could not reach the nectar?
Perhaps
They are my brethren
The existential failures
Who died centuries ago
Metonymy of keratin
A hidden Pentecost
With one resolution
That gestates during the centuries
And glistens like scaly reminders
Of fish with feet
Drink to your swollen appendix
And starve the hungry
Because these flops are liminal
Like whiskey and oracles
A holding environment which is not one thing
Or the other

Beggars gesture between the stars

They drift and gesture
Like hideous sponges
And they cannot be restored
But the beggars know more
Celestial lepers
That congregate
And plead for a new evolution
A new messiah
With steel robes
And a new hierarchy
And a scepter
To judge the innocent

Reverse eschatology

There may be a secret in the rejected words
Just like the birds with small beaks
Who cannot reach the nectar
There might be wisdom in the early deaths
And needless car accidents
A veritable bible etched
On the mobile home walls of an obese woman
Who died of heat death in Arizona
Anthems and instructions ring out
From dead Black boys
And wasted water
From a young disabled woman in a wheelchair
And abandoned buildings in Baltimore whisper
And become the anvil of the universe
To forge something new and sublime
A translucent jelly
Which has more potential than anything
That has ever existed

Ammonia and turpentine

Ammonia and turpentine
Bleach and tar
Vegetable oil, paint thinner and soap
Form a celestial river
Where plaster becomes paper
And fiberglass melts into plastic
Laminate the spaces
Between the stars
And fill every black hole with gasoline
We cannot build a universe
But we can clean one
A cartography of garbage and billions of years of evolution
Soaked in whiskey and jelly
Is divine
Pray to it like a rank god
To deliver you from boredom

Human soil

I read a poem by a man I did not know
His words moved me more
Than a million hit songs and entrepreneurs
Grace, beauty and history
Planted themselves in human soil
And no policy could stop their growth
No court decision could arrest them
Instead
I was transported to a boat in the middle of the ocean
Where I saw a lighthouse
Like the skeleton of the waves

Everything

Everything I have ever dreamed of or remembered
Exists somewhere
Continually hammered
On an abandoned anvil
Like an autumnal plague
With its reoccurrence of Enlightenment
And the cartilage of atoms
But this is all premature
We are not ready

Rebuild the Messiah

At Lowes, there are aisles stocked with disinfectants
Various cleaners, bleaches
Spray bottles
Industrial solvents
And air purifiers
Fertilizers and concrete
All these things flower symmetrically in the rows
And
Shopping carts become like messiahs
To deliver us from a terror as yet unknown
But terror grows mutates in the linoleum
And all of the things you thought were safe and clean
Showed their relentless evil
Terror in the eyes of the pretty cashier
And the rent-a-truck
In the soda bottles and lumber
It waits
For us to name it

It did not have to happen to this way

It did not have to happen to this way
Each shadow and breath
Fell in a specific direction
Corners became guides
And pained arrows
Messiahs

Accountability as helium

There is a curriculum in the sun
And the paving truck in my neighbor's driveway
Curricular objectives burn in the grass
On an August afternoon
Paint and molding can be a teacher of sorts
As they line the hall
But there is also a curriculum in dreams
In the honey-sweet walls which drip
In the later afternoon of those dreams
And spill into the sun
And
All the curriculums melt into one

My friends

The machines run
And hum a hymn of progress
As they produce
Steel creatures
Huge and unhappy
Bleeding and lonely
The creatures do not notice me
The creatures live in the rain
Grotesque unhappy things
Produced infinitely
Monotonously they sweep the garage floor
And watch reruns of commercials
And mouth the words to them

You have done it 6 times before (that I know of)

The mothers joke about giving head
And laugh at the ones that don't
In the hot July afternoon
Shirts collect sweat
And the green beans turned warm
There are oil tanks and broken dehumidifiers
And the planned obsolescence of oral sex
And marriage, of cheap plastic forks
And clueless cats that watch birds behind a screen
Oral sex does not make children
Turn around and do it again
Blessed deviance of July
Of chlorine bleach
To scrub the morality clean
(Just jump in the pool it doubles as a baptismal font)

Progress mapped onto tombs

Black sarcophagus
Spent like fuel
The vortex is suspended
At the zenith marking
Gasoline rivers that Vespucci never explored
He should have stopped
Turned the boat around
And not named the rocks and canyons
There are no more bullets
And no more batteries
No more jalopies or gold
The hills are the only metaverse
We will ever need

Ingested the life which dies

You have swallowed gallons of starlight
But in a different form
Your backside
Is also a star
Mapped into soft female flesh
Worn
Like our morals and deviance
Erect a lighthouse here
Erect a marker
To guide us through a world
Without comfort of gods
And named stars
There is only a hot smell
Which yields no children,
But only yields enlightenment, only infinity
At night
With the windows open
And the children are asleep
We have created
A new cartography

The same end

It's the same modes
It's the same mirrors
Splayed across
The electric glass
When each grain of sand
Claims to be exemplary
But all are equally useless without each other
Drain the gasoline from all the faces and containers
So no one is accountable

Thinking about the end (drinking poem)

Think I am going to drink tonight
There is a crusty rubber stopper in my foot
Pull it
Make room for Southern Comfort
Drain it
Do you love me?
I know you have had better and I don't care
Drain me of everything
Squeeze my appendix
Through the hole in my foot
Step on it
Juice trail on the pavement
That follows me forever
Drink to that
Fuck I woke up again
I hate the people, my friends
But they love their clown
Hanging from the sun
So everyone can see
Tonsil useless appendix
But it will incinerate hanging clowns
With holes in their feet
Big breasted alcohol drunks and
Berating defunct steroid gods
Living on prison earth
Looking for bitches to violate
Cowering behind toilets
With big red noses
Incinerate the planet
Listen to the president
And prison gods with big hands
Listen to the leaders
Use the sun as a bomb
Drive it into the mouth
Of a silent clown
Now hanging from the circus tent

Ballast

Pacing in the aisle
Trying to fill it
The mouth with nails or sawdust maybe
Anything to weight me down
Securely
Invisible gales wash through the pathways
Sweep me like kites
Or balloons or confetti
Into the blue sky
Oblivions divide like cancer
In the jaw
Black holes that drop to the feet
With the weight of their own gravity
Send me spiraling
I grab hold of metal shelves
Trying to keep myself
On this planet
I am too light and
Can feel my blood
Blown through the sun
Into that terrible star
But suddenly in the store
Jackals behind the pens and notebooks
Demons in the light fixtures
Maggots and lice on the floor hear the call
And crawl into my empty bones for me, for weight

Receptacle

He scours the universe
Looking for stars and Nissans or whatever
All for me
Plastic lines the heart
I am pumped with tar
And blood
And rotten fish
And all of the things he finds
they overflow out of my mouth
But still
He will not unhook the pump in my back
All of the things he collects from the universe
Get pumped into me

We are the only thing left (Objective End)

We are the only thing left
The remnant
The residue
Of a failed attempt
There was more at one time long ago
Now
There are just embers and sawdust
On a concrete floor
And even these were only a dream
Of lonely stupid men
Who slept in corners
Where the universe joins
But they were still oblivious

We should have seen it sooner (Subjective End)

The tired man sits at the bar
And finishes his drink
He has a stain on his shirt
After the last sip he sighs and leaves.

The door opens and a gust of wind
Nearly blows his hat off
On the walk home
He is accompanied only
By the falling snow.

He unlocks the door to his home and enters
Sitting in darkness he drifts in and out of sleep
Hoping there is something more.

Acknowledgments

The poems *Here at the end* and *A Room in the Sun* first appeared in the publication AHF Magazine.

The poem *Ballast* first appeared in the publication Black Petals.

www.ingramcontent.com/pod-product-compliance
Lightning Source LLC
Chambersburg PA
CBHW072106110526
44590CB00018B/3334